BRITAIN IN OLD PHOTOGRAPHS

AROUND
EASTBOURNE

PAT BERRY &
KEVIN GORDON

SUTTON PUBLISHING LIMITED

Sutton Publishing Limited
Phoenix Mill · Thrupp · Stroud
Gloucestershire · GL5 2BU

First published 1996

Cover photographs: (front) soldiers outside the
Welcome Hut at Summerdown Military
Convalescent Camp during the First World
War; (back) a cheery Eastbourne postcard.

British Library Cataloguing in Publication Data
A catalogue record for this book is available from the
British Library.

ISBN 0-7509-1272-3

Typeset in 10/12 Perpetua.
Typesetting and origination by
Sutton Publishing Limited.
Printed in Great Britain by
Ebenezer Baylis, Worcester.

CONTENTS

Motcombe Gardens. This is the source of the Bourne stream which gave Eastbourne its name. The pond which was within the grounds of Motcombe Farm (*see* p. 82) was lined and enclosed in 1857, and two years later the newly formed Eastbourne Waterworks Company laid pipes from the pond to supply a reservoir in Susans Road. The course of the stream is now mainly enclosed from the pond and runs underground to the rear of the houses in Moy Avenue and from there to Gilbert Lake in Princes Park.

INTRODUCTION

It is seven years since Cecile Woodford's Eastbourne collection was published in the *Britain in Old Photographs* series, and there have been several other similar volumes. Readers might be forgiven for wondering if there is anything left worth printing, but we hope our book will prove that there is. The development of Eastbourne as a holiday resort coincided with the wider availability of photography, so there has never been any shortage of views of the town and its people. Old postcards can still be found at fairs and in antique shops around the world, and many of those we have collected are appearing here in print for the first time.

Material from several unique sources is also included: Kevin's family has lived in the area for at least five generations and he has access not only to albums and photographs but also to his grandmother's Commonplace Books, wherein she gathered newspaper cuttings, poems, and her own memoirs of local events.

The last section of this book, 'Eastbourne by Night', is devoted to views taken by local musician and photographer Mr Ellis Kelsey and discovered only recently in the attic of his last home, in Seaford. The original lantern slides, about one hundred years old, were skilfully transferred to film by Brian Taylor of Seaford Museum. The omission of detailed captions in this section is deliberate, so that you can concentrate on the difficulties overcome and the patience needed to produce these studies – you can almost hear the silence! The titles are Mr Kelsey's own.

The town and resort of Eastbourne, with a resident population of 88,000, has grown out of the separate communities of Meads, Sea Houses, South Bourne and East Bourne (Old Town). Under the various section headings we have tried to include old views of all four, at the same time showing some of the more recent past, in which readers may find themselves or their ancestors, or events they recall. However, errors and omissions may have crept in and we would be delighted to hear from anyone who wishes to write to us, care of our publishers.

Many of the streets and buildings illustrated herein have changed little over the years since they were photographed. One way to appreciate this aspect of our heritage is to walk where the famous have walked and imagine their impressions. T.E. Lawrence, for instance, came to 18 Southfields Road to consult C.M. Doughty, an eminent authority on Arabian affairs. Mabel Lucie Attwell, the children's artist, knew the Ocklynge area during her tenancy of the Manor House. Richard Jefferies, the Victorian naturalist and writer, visited the town and was fascinated by the downland wildlife.

We hope you will gain as much pleasure from reading this book as we had in compiling it. May it enhance your knowledge of the town and, who knows?, lead you along hitherto unexplored paths to interesting discoveries about the history of your own family or home.

Pat Berry and Kevin Gordon
1996

SEAFRONT

'All aboard the Skylark.' The Allchorn family owned the well-known pleasure boat, the Skylark, seen here
in about 1905 taking aboard visitors, probably for a trip around the Beachy Head lighthouse. Pleasure
boats were run during the summer by local fishermen who had to wear ribbons in their caps to show that they
were licensed by the local authority.

Rough seas at the Redoubt. In 1867 the Redoubt Fortress was owned by the War Department who spent £10,000 on building a sea wall around the fort. Like the area near the Queens Hotel, this became known as a 'splash point' where high tides attracted crowds to watch the sea.

The bandstand on Marine Parade. The 'birdcage' bandstand was erected by Eastbourne Council in 1894 at a cost of £300. In 1922 it was moved to the Redoubt Gardens but the concrete foundations can still be seen at this site. Eridge's bathing machine office is on the right.

The 'birdcage' bandstand in place at the Redoubt Music Gardens, 1923. The bandstand was equipped with lighting. The Electric Light Company was formed in 1882 and pioneered street lighting in the south of England. Many towns, including Dublin, sent representatives to Eastbourne to see the lights; the Chinese Ambassador T'Seng was present at the opening of the company's works in Junction Road in 1885.

The new Redoubt bandstand, c. 1937. In the 1930s the 'birdcage' was replaced by a new bandstand and sun lounge. Here a large crowd has gathered in the Music Gardens and on the ramparts of the Redoubt to watch a beauty contest organized by the *Daily Mirror*.

Pier diver. For a fee of 6*d*, and under the supervision of a 'Pier Master', gentlemen bathers could plunge into the Channel from a board on the eastern side of the pier. It was also the venue for the Eastern Swimming Club which met here between 6 and 8 a.m. during the summer months. Nobody is on the beach in this view so the water must have been cold for the diver.

Games saloons on the pier, 1904. The American bowling saloon and the rifle saloon with electric targets were added to the pier in 1901. At this time the pier had its own orchestra, and the notice in the centre is advertising a 3 p.m. matinée in the pavilion. At the top of the building was a camera obscura, where in a darkened room an image of the sea-front was reflected on to a table for visitors to view. This was once the largest in Britain.

Eastbourne Pier was built between 1866 and 1870 by Eugenius Birch, who was also responsible for the piers in Blackpool, Brighton and Hastings. On New Year's Day 1877 the shoreward end was destroyed in a storm and was re-built at a higher level, as seen in this Edwardian view.

The pier tea-room, 1950s. The first pavilion at the end of the pier could accommodate four hundred people and was built in 1888 at a cost of £250. It was replaced in 1899 by the 'Kursaal', a visitors' centre in the style of other watering-places, with a theatre, bars, offices and a tea-room offering views across the Channel.

The pier entrance. The kiosk on the left is a Maynard's sweet shop with advertisements for Fry's Mineral Water. The kiosk on the right is run by Aylesbury's Dairy. The central pay-booth charges 2*d* for entrance and the pier attractions include an 'Al-fresco concert', 'The Girls of Gothenburg' and 'Animated Pictures'.

This view shows the new, taller kiosks which in 1912 replaced the round ones shown above. In the foreground is a rank for bath-chairs, and electric lights have been erected around the Carpet Gardens. The right-hand kiosk was later used as the booking office for Chapman's Coaches, who ran tours in the area.

The white hoardings in use to keep the public away from the pavilion being built at the shoreward end of the pier dates this picture to 1924. Built as a music pavilion, it is now known as the Blue Room. The full length of the pier – 1,000 ft – together with its landing stage can be seen in this aerial view.

Louis Levy was a French photographer who published postcards from offices in Paris and Holborn, London. Each card was numbered and included his initials, LL. He produced over 120 views of Eastbourne and this one from 1907 shows traders on a warm day on the Lower Parade, whilst on the beach a large crowd has gathered to watch some entertainers.

The Promenade hackney carriage stand. This hackney carriage stand was in Grand Parade opposite Hartington Place. There were three classes of hackney carriage: the largest, drawn by one or two horses or mules, could seat up to five people; a smaller carriage, pulled by a pony or mule, could convey up to three people; while the smallest type was drawn by an ass or goat and could take up to two children. Prices depended on time or distance, which were carefully measured by the Surveyor of the Local Board.

The Burlington Hotel, 1937. Built in 1851, this was the first large hotel to be built on the seafront and was named after the 2nd Earl of Burlington (later the 7th Duke of Devonshire). The building on the far left is 22 Grand Parade, which was acquired by the Burlington Hotel in 1929. In 1860 it housed a school run by Thomas Hopley who, on 21 April that year, beat a pupil, Reginald Cancellor, so severely that he died. In July Hopley was convicted of manslaughter at Lewes and sentenced to four years' imprisonment.

The Carpet Gardens have been a feature of the seafront opposite the Burlington Hotel for over one hundred years. In this view from the turn of the century, visitors stroll along Grand Parade with no need to worry about traffic.

Bathing machines were first recorded at Scarborough in 1735 and were being used at Brighton in 1750. For a fee, bathers could change into their costumes in private and, after the device had been pulled into the sea by a horse, could step discreetly straight into the water. Some bathing machine proprietors offered swimming lessons.

The old bandstand was built between 1883 and 1884 and was used by Eastbourne's own Municipal Band as well as by visiting bands. On the left is a cigar kiosk with a distinctive sign above.

The new bandstand was opened in 1935 and could seat three thousand people. As can be seen, it became hugely popular with visitors. An electric notice shows that programme 4 is being played by a Scottish military band.

This postcard view, taken from the top of the pier pavilion, shows the Wish Tower and the coastguard station, high up on Beachy Head. A horse can be seen pulling a bathing machine into the sea. This postcard was sent by Mrs Wilson to her grocer in Blackburn and lists the shopping she would like to be delivered on her return from holiday in Eastbourne.

Bathing machines fell out of use during the 1920s and were replaced by bathing tents and bathing huts, many of which were converted from the old machines. The Wish Tower was the last but one of a line of Martello towers built between Folkestone and Seaford in 1803 when Napoleon was threatening to invade England. The low-lying land around it was a marshy area known as the 'wash' or 'wish', hence the name.

Until the turn of the century when the lifeboat house was built, the lifeboat was launched from the beach near the rear of the Leaf Hall. Here, the *James Stevens No. 6* has been run out from the William Terriss Memorial Lifeboat House for inspection by the summer crowds. This lifeboat was in service between 1899 and 1924; it was launched forty-three times and saved thirty-four souls.

In 1902 a corrugated iron boathouse was built at the fishing station near Princes Park and in 1937 the William Terriss building became the world's first lifeboat museum. Here, Kevin and his brother Andrew watch the lifeboat crew at work on the *Beryl Tollemache*. This lifeboat rescued a total of 154 people over a twenty-eight year career, which came to an end in 1977.

The paddle-steamer *Empress of India* leaving the pier in the early 1930s. The bathing machines have gone and instead people relax in deckchairs marked 'BoE', provided by the Borough of Eastbourne.

Can you date this view of the parade and pier? The answer is on the next page.

In 1966 the director George Sidney chose Eastbourne as the location for the seaside scenes in the Paramount film *Half a Sixpence*. This musical version of H.G. Wells' story *Kipps* starred Tommy Steele, Julia Foster, Cyril Ritchard and James Villiers. A number of local people were employed as extras; they are seen above during a tea-break. Once again the beach was full of bathing machines and the parades resounded to the sound of horse-drawn vehicles. The pleasure craft even had false funnels fitted to complete the Edwardian seaside atmosphere. (From original colour slides by Mr Roger Gordon)

STREET SCENES

Many local traders used to deliver to the door. This fishmonger, known as 'Fishy', delivered fresh fish twice a week to homes in the Redoubt area. He is seen here outside 'Beulah', 15 Taddington Road, as Kevin's great-grandfather, Ebenezer Roberts, clears snow on a cold day in 1915.

South Street was once the route of an open sewer called Shomer Dyke which emptied into the sea near the Wish Tower. Nearby, a toy and pleasure fair was held yearly on 12 March but by 1819 this had dwindled away. St Saviour's Church (behind the trees) was built on a turnip field which had been part of the 7th Duke of Devonshire's land.

South Terrace and Cornfield Road, 1910. Following the unveiling of the war memorial in 1920 this area became Memorial Square, now a busy junction. The large tree on the left was planted by Princess Alice, the second daughter of Queen Victoria, on one of her many visits to the town. The large villa on the right for a long time housed the offices of Edgar Horn, auctioneers.

This part of Seaside Road is now known as Trinity Trees. On the left is Togni and Ferrari's café restaurant, the site later occupied by the Co-op. In the foreground a handbarrow holds baskets marked 'Campbells', and a coach and four is passing John Nix, jewellers, at 6 Terminus Road.

Upperton Road. It would be impossible to take a similar photograph today without traffic. On the right is Station Terrace with Proctor's the chemist. On the far right two men have stopped to talk outside Ricketts' coal merchants at the entrance to the railway goods yard. In the centre the shops of the imposing Terminus Buildings include Pickford's travel bureau and Pawson's confectioners.

Terminus Road, looking north towards the railway station, 1904. The Midland Bank now occupies the site of Tyrells on the left. Just behind the Brighton Arms public house are the awnings of Arthur and Co., tobacconists. The grand building on the right is 115 Terminus Road, occupied by Barclays Bank. It was built in 1895 for the Lewes Old Bank, which was absorbed into Barclays Bank the following year. It was topped with a prominent green dome which was visible for miles around, but an enemy bomb destroyed the building in March 1943. On the extreme right are the premises of C. Towner, estate agents.

This deserted street scene shows Terminus Road at the junction of Langney Road, 1904. On the left is Edwin Smith & Son, drapers, who had several shops in the area; next door is Bradford's coal merchants and beyond, at no. 36, is T. Knight & Co., furnishers and general ironmongers. These shops were formerly Bobby & Co. (see pp. 55 and 79) and are now Debenhams.

Victoria Place. This is now the southern end of Terminus Road. On the left behind the trees stood the smart Victoria Mansions. On the right, two slot machines stand outside the entrance to the Royal Victoria Baths where a hot sea-water bath could be had for 1s 6d. The proprietor also advertised that hot and cold sea-water could be delivered and that 'Ozone' baths were available for 3s.

Elms Avenue. Built close to the pier on the site of The Elms and part of Susans Farmhouse, this road was principally occupied by boarding houses and apartments, as shown on the notice on the house on the left.

Cavendish Place, 1913. Cavendish was the family name of the Dukes of Devonshire. Cavendish Place was formerly called North Street. The German industrialist Friedrich Engels, who collaborated with Karl Marx in producing *The Communist Manifesto* and *Das Kapital*, spent several holidays at 4 Cavendish Place. After his death in 1895 his ashes were scattered over the sea from Beachy Head. Note the two well-dressed children with hoops.

Seaside, 1905. This view, looking north-east towards the chimney of the refuse destructor works in St Phillip's Avenue, shows the tower of the Leaf Hall on the right. Formerly the Workmen's Hall, the building was opened in 1864 with money donated by Mr William Leaf. It was designed by R.K. Blessley who also designed the Grand Hotel and St John's Church in Polegate.

Susans Road, 1910. This road was named after Mr Susan's farm, which was built of flint in 1714 and stood at the Seaside Road end. This view is from the top of the Wesleyan Church which stands on the corner of Pevensey Road. At the end of the road can be seen the railway line and some carriages, with Cavendish Road bridge to the right of All Souls' Church tower.

Wilmington Gardens, 1908. This road, off Carlisle Road and opposite the Winter Gardens, was named after Spencer Compton, Earl of Wilmington. This photograph was taken from where the Congress Theatre now stands and three horse-drawn cabs can be seen waiting in front of a cabman's shelter.

Meads Road, near the junction with Granville Road, 1905. This tree-lined road led into Meads from the Town Hall. On the left a girl stands at the entrance to St Peter's Church (*see* p. 61) as a small cart trundles down the road. The pavements were an attractive feature of many Eastbourne streets, and the brick paviors used were probably made at Messrs Norman's works at Chailey.

Meads Street. The world's first municipal bus service began operating on 12 April 1903 between here and the railway station. In this picture someone is hurrying to catch one of the Corporation's fourteen-seat Milnes-Daimler buses. The cottages on the right have now been replaced by Meads Court, while the new Ship Hotel replaced a seventeenth-century inn of the same name which stood further up the road.

Meads Street, 1919. On the left is Dalton Road and, on the corner, Hammicks bakery at 1 Meads Street. The next two shops are occupied by Harold Parker's, ironmongers, then Potter's fishmongers. The last shop is the Meads Library, who published this postcard view.

Meads Village. This small community was built in 1894 by George Wallis and was known locally as Wallis's Cottages. Wallis was the local agent for the Duke of Devonshire and in 1866 became Eastbourne's first mayor. The houses have their gardens in the centre of the square.

The Albemarle Hotel. Until the turn of the century this was known as the Old Anchor Hotel and an anchor can still be seen above the main entrance. To the left is the Albion Hotel, which was built in 1821 as a town house for the Earl of Ashburnham; it was the first house in Eastbourne to be lit by electricity and the first to be fitted with a telephone. To the right of the hotel, in the lower view, are 27 and 28 Marine Parade, which were built in 1840 and have Doric columns supporting their balconies.

TRANSPORT

Open-top bus in Terminus Road, c. 1908. The omnibus from Hampden Park has just arrived outside the Gildredge Hotel, near the railway station. The conductor waits at the bottom of the steps. The advertisement on the bus is for James Andrews, sculptor and mason of Gore Park. By 1910 there were twenty-three open-top double-decker buses in the County Borough's fleet.

Eastbourne.

Dear

J've had a Ripping Time.
Have just got

left, and my Return Half

L. B. & S. C. Rly.

EASTBOURNE

TO

WHERE I CUM FROM

So J'm coming Home.

Yours,

The Brighton to Hastings railway by-passed
Eastbourne and until May 1849 passengers from
the town had to travel by Mr Daniel Burford's bus
to Polegate to catch the train. The present station
is the fourth and was built in 1886. The comic
postcard (left) shows a representation of a silver
sixpence and a London, Brighton & South Coast
Railway ticket.

Southern Railway's locomotive no. 914 'Eastbourne' was named after the town. A 4–4–0 Schools class (V) engine built in 1932, by the time it was broken up in 1961 it had travelled over a million miles. Here it leaves Stewarts Lane depot in south London for jubilee celebrations in Eastbourne.

On 19 March 1967 'Wincanton', a West Country class engine, no. 34108, pulled into platform 1 of Eastbourne station. A crowd of some 400 people, including Alec Gordon, Kevin's grandfather (centre, facing camera), gathered to see this, the last steam train to visit Eastbourne. The train's visit was organized by the Southern Counties Touring Society, whose secretary Mr W. Crawford from Wallington, Surrey, was also the guard of the train.

Vinall's charabanc departs from the seafront in 1925. The driver in his distinctive white cap is William Vinall who lived at a house called Woodlands in Arlington (below). He actually built the coach himself and took holidaymakers from Eastbourne to the local countryside; a convenient stop was usually made at his home where his wife Alice (Kevin's great-great-aunt) ran a tea garden. A round trip of 25 miles included 'a good tea' and cost 3s 6d. William also ran football special coaches to London. The company was later taken over by Chapman's Coaches.

Eastbourne bus girls, *c.* 1916. Owing to the number of men in the Forces during the First World War, many occupations previously held only by men became open for women for the first time. This picture was taken by the Rembrandt Studios of Langney Road, Eastbourne.

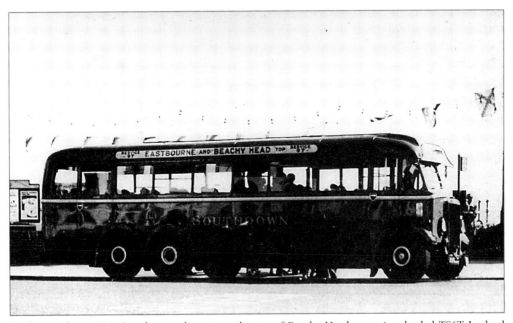

Eastbourne bus, 1934. For the popular trip to the top of Beachy Head, two six-wheeled TS6T Leyland Tiger single-decker buses with folding roofs were licensed to convey a maximum of forty seated passengers per trip, eight more than the normal capacity of these buses. Originally petrol-driven, they were converted to diesel in 1940 and kept in service till 1952, with the seating capacity reduced to thirty-nine.

M. Henri Salmet sits in his 50 hp Bleriot monoplane during the *Daily Mail*-sponsored British Isles aeroplane circuit tour, entitled 'Wake Up, England', in 1912. The tour was designed to promote air travel. Salmet was the holder of the British record for altitude (9,000 ft), as well as the London to Paris speed record (3 hours 12 minutes) and the overseas record (Eastbourne to Dieppe, 80 miles).

In the summer of 1912 a hangar enclosure was built to the east of the pier to house two seaplanes which were taking part in the *Daily Mail* tour. The pilots were Claude Grahame-White and James Travers who offered short flights for 5 guineas per person per trip. One passenger was the writer H.G. Wells, then holidaying in Eastbourne, who reportedly enjoyed his flight.

Leroy's aeroplane delivery service! Leroy's radio shop was situated next to the Astolat tea-rooms in Cornfield Road (*see* p. 54). On 29 August 1934 Leroy's had their 1935 radio models flown into the Wilmington Aero Club as a publicity stunt.

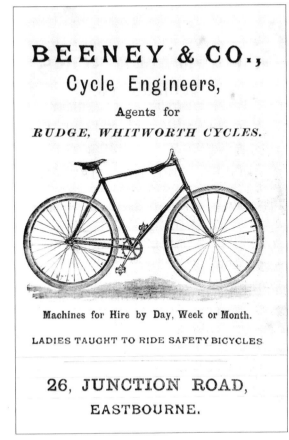

BEENEY & CO.,

Cycle Engineers,

Agents for

RUDGE, WHITWORTH CYCLES.

Machines for Hire by Day, Week or Month.

LADIES TAUGHT TO RIDE SAFETY BICYCLES.

26, JUNCTION ROAD,

EASTBOURNE.

Advertisement for Beeneys bicycle engineers. Travelling by bicycle became popular after the introduction of the safety machine at the turn of the century. Opportunities for leisure cycling were afforded by the local cycling club and the laying down of a track at Devonshire Park.

Bath-chair stand, 1905. Eastbourne, a town visited by many invalids and convalescents, boasted several places where bath-chairs and attendants could be hired. The passenger was seated in the cab and the attendant pulled the chair along by a long metal handle, or the passenger could hold and control the handle if he preferred. The local authority issued licences and stipulated where the stands should be, and they were indicated by metal plates bearing the initials BCS.

Many pleasure steamers called at Eastbourne's pier on their trips along the south coast; they included the *Empress of India*, the *Ravenswood* and the *Waverley*. Another visitor was the *Brighton Queen II* which sailed from Eastbourne during the 1930s, and was sunk at Dunkirk in 1940 during the evacuation of British troops.

MARITIME

The Royal Sovereign *lightship was situated 7 miles south of the coast at Royal Sovereign Shoal, named after a warship that was wrecked here in 1757. The lightship was placed at this spot in April 1875 and was replaced by the light tower in 1972.*

Beachy Head, 1880s. The name Beachy Head is probably derived from the Norman/French *beau-chef* ('fair-head'). The summit is 575 ft above sea-level. This view shows some of the seven chalk pillars called the Churles or the Charleses. Coastal erosion has seen the loss of these magnificent parts of our coastal scenery.

Beachy Head lighthouse, 1902. Belle-Tout lighthouse, on the clifftop near Birling Gap, was often obscured by low cloud, so in 1899 work began on a new lighthouse at sea-level. A dam was built around the site and foundations sunk 18 ft into the chalk. The lighthouse is made of Cornish granite and materials were sent down on an aerial ropeway which can be seen at top right. This picture was taken before the lantern was added. The building was opened in October 1902 and manned until 1983 when it became fully automated. The chalk outcrop to the right of the lighthouse was known as the Devil's Chimney.

On the evening of Saturday 14 May 1904 the German schooner *Emma Louise*, with a cargo of china clay, ran into thick fog while en route from Charlestown to Hamburg and went aground about 200 yd to the west of Beachy Head lighthouse, suffering some damage on her starboard side. A rocket line was fired from the clifftop to the vessel, but it could not be secured by the six men of the crew. However, they and their skipper were later taken off by the Newhaven lifeboat, and the schooner was refloated on the high tide next morning and towed to Newhaven.

Eastfield.
Stranded - Beachy Head
Dec.3.09.

On the night of 2/3 December 1909, the 2,300-ton tramp steamer SS *Eastfield* ran aground in a gale some 200 yd on the Eastbourne side of Belle-Tout. Less than ten years old and recently returned from a three month voyage to Borneo, she was sailing in ballast from Hull to Barry with twenty-one crew and a stowaway. At the next low tide the crew disembarked and walked along the beach to Birling Gap, while their belongings were hauled up the cliff face by block and tackle, as seen below. Three weeks later, the vessel managed to go under its own steam to Tilbury.

On Saturday 16 March 1912 the four-masted P&O liner *Oceana* and the German sailing ship *Pisagua* collided off Beachy Head. Four of the *Oceana*'s lifeboats were swept away. One of the boats that went to the aid of the stricken vessel included the London, Brighton & South Coast Railway ferry *Sussex*. Deck boy Ted Davis (above), together with an officer, despite some personal risk, helped transfer survivors to the cross-channel steamer, and the *Oceana* finally sank seven hours afterwards (left). Ted was later summoned to London to give evidence at an enquiry into the accident. He was paid 11s 2d expenses and given a six-course lunch for his trouble.

The Eastbourne lifeboat *James Stevens* was launched within a quarter of an hour of the collision between the *Oceana* and the *Pisagua*; it saved twenty passengers and crew. The survivors, including this little boy and Ginger, the ship's cat, were taken to the pier and thence to the Albion Hotel and the Leaf Hall.

S.S. HERCULES. AFTER COLLISION OFF EASTBOURNE. JUNE 4TH 1911
PHOTO. COOPER.

In thick fog 9 miles off Beachy Head on Saturday 4 June 1911 at 5.30 p.m., the 3,960-ton *Hercules* of Bilbao, sailing from Pensacola (Florida) to Holland with a cargo of timber, collided with the vessel *Ariadne* of Rotterdam, en route from Seaham to Toulon. Early the next day the *Hercules*, her starboard bow severely damaged, was towed by the Bristol Navigation Company's cargo steamer *Juno* to within ¼ mile of Eastbourne's Grand Parade. Spectators crowded the sea-front while others took to small craft for a closer look. Eventually both vessels were towed to Dover for repair.

The unscheduled visit of HMS *London*, Friday 17 May 1913. Commissioned in 1902, this third-class battleship of 15,000 tons, with Captain E. Grafton and a crew of 800, anchored 2 miles off Eastbourne. The captain's daughter was a pupil at Clovelly-Kepplestone School, Meads (*see* p. 70). On the Saturday all the girls and a number of the school staff were invited to join the *London*'s 'make and mend' afternoon, with luncheon, tea and deck games. This postcard was purchased by one of the girls who made the visit.

This plaque, unveiled on 24 October 1914 by the singer Clara Butt, is to be found opposite the central bandstand. The inscription reads: 'This tablet is erected as a tribute to the self-sacrifice and devotion of John Wesley Woodward (formerly a member of the Eastbourne Municipal Orchestra, the Duke of Devonshire's Orchestra and the Grand Hotel, Eastbourne, Orchestra) who, with others of the hero musicians of the ship's band, perished in the Atlantic through the sinking of the White Star liner *Titanic* on April 15th, 1912. Faithful unto death.'

In April 1919 the foot of Baily's Brow, the sixth of the Seven Sisters cliffs (counting from west to east) was the scene of a remarkable event. Since November 1916 the wreck of the tramp steamer *Oushla* had been stranded there and at the end of the First World War, the German submarine UB211 was being taken to France as 'spoils of war' when the tow-line broke and the submarine ran ashore, its bow jamming into the *Oushla*'s boiler-room. For many years the remains were readily identifiable and a few vestiges can still be found.

On the evening of Sunday 20 October 1968, some 15 miles off Beachy Head, a number of explosions occurred aboard the 15,500-ton Norwegian tanker *Sitakund*. The vessel, in ballast from Wilhelmshaven to Libya, caught fire and four of her crew of forty-three were lost. The remainder were taken off and the British Rail Newhaven tug *Meeching* took the furiously burning ship in tow. After a hazardous voyage towards the resort, with the Eastbourne and Newhaven lifeboats as well as the fire brigade standing by, the tanker anchored a mile off Holywell. She remained there for nearly three months till the sounder parts could be towed away. Not till 1972 were the last dangerous pieces broken up with explosive charges. (Photograph reproduced by kind permission of the editor of the *Sussex Express*)

PEOPLE & EVENTS

Elizabeth Quill (known as Kitty) was a popular figure who sold flowers on the middle parade between the Wish Tower and the Bandstand. After selling some flowers to the Princess of Wales she fixed a 'by appointment' badge to her basket.

Eastbourne has welcomed many Royal visitors. Edward VII visited the town in July 1903 and here his carriage is in Grove Road, en route from the railway station to the Town Hall. Hope & Co., gents' outfitters (in the background) are still trading but are now in premises on the other side of the road. Behind the cyclist is M. & M. Phillips, dressmakers, and further down the road the (Strict) Baptist Chapel.

Like many Sussex towns and villages, Eastbourne celebrated 5 November with gusto. Here, members of the St Mary's Bonfire Society pose in front of their banner in 1906. Kevin's great-grandfather, Ebenezer Roberts, is dressed as the judge in the centre; a deeply religious man, he attended the (Strict) Baptist Chapel and delivered the anti-Catholic bonfire speeches at the society's bonfire site off the East Dean Road.

The 1899 lifeboat house. In 1897 William Terriss, a popular actor specializing in nautical roles, was assassinated at the stage door of the Adelphi Theatre. The *Daily Telegraph* organized a memorial fund, and the money was used to build the boathouse (above). On 22 March 1937, in the presence of William's daughter, Falkland Islands-born actress Ellaline Terriss (right), the boathouse was officially opened as the country's first permanent lifeboat museum.

On 7 February 1906 the Duke of Norfolk, who was not only Lord Lieutenant of Sussex but also a major of the Second Battalion of the Royal Sussex Regiment, travelled to Eastbourne to unveil the Royal Sussex Regiment memorial opposite the pier. A guard of honour formed by the regiment, in their smart red and blue uniforms, had travelled to Eastbourne by a special train from Chichester. The ceremony was attended by over 4,000 people and contingents of Naval, Artillery and Engineer Volunteers, Sussex Yeomanry and Cadet Corps. A local photographer was on the scene ready to produce postcards the following day. This one was posted on 9 February.

Sir Ernest Henry Shackleton (1874–1922). Sir Ernest, who lived in Meads, commanded the British Antarctic Expedition in 1907–8, reaching a latitude of 88° 23' south, at that time one hundred miles nearer the South Pole than man had previously attained. Sir Ernest was knighted in 1909 and commanded a second Antarctic expedition in 1914–17, which involved him in feats of great courage and endurance. His vessel, the Quest, anchored off Eastbourne in September 1921 at the start of his third expedition, just as the Nimrod and the Endurance had done before his earlier voyages. He reached South Georgia Island on 4 January 1922, but died the next day and was buried on the island.

The 'Great Blizzard'. The snows of December 1908 only lasted for three days but were sufficient to cause considerable disruption in the town. Borough employees, supplemented with unemployed workers, toiled through the night to open blocked roads and clear pavements. Only one injury was recorded: a borough foreman checking on the work being done slipped and broke his knee.

The Roberts family. This studio portrait by R.W. Vieler of 19 Elms Buildings shows Kevin's grandmother Bessie with her parents, Ebenezer and Bessie Emily Roberts (née Bennett). Ebenezer attended the National School, Eastbourne, but appeared in the 1881 census at the age of 13 as a 'driver of goats'. He married in Cavendish Place chapel in 1894. Religion and law were of great interest to him and he was for many years sick visitor for the local branch of the Manchester Unity of Oddfellows who met at the Leaf Hall. A keen amateur poet, he commemorated many occasions in verse, and a small collection was published by his daughter.

This is the statue of the 8th Duke of Devonshire photographed in the studio of Alfred Drury ARA before it was moved to the Western Lawns for the unveiling on 24 October 1910. The picture is taken from a postcard purchased by Sarah Powell who, with her friend Janie McBirnie, witnessed the Duke of Norfolk performing the ceremony.

In the mid-1880s the 7th Duke of Devonshire funded the creation of the parades between Holywell and the Wish Tower, later to be named Dukes Drive after him. Here the terracing is shown under construction; 400,000 cubic yards of chalk and greensand stone had to be removed in the process. The large building on the right was known locally as 'Earp's Folly' (*see* p. 69).

WILL IT COME TO THIS?

THE EASTBOURNE MAN HUNT. 7884 MORE WOMEN THAN MEN.

Cartoonists like J.W. Davis entertained readers of local newspapers with their visual comments on fashion and events at the turn of the century. These two speak for themselves.

EXTRACT FROM
EASTBOURNE CENSUS RETURN :
"THE FIGURES ARE EXTRAORDINARY."

Astolat's tea rooms, *c.* 1930. Food was prepared in the kitchen of the premises at 37 Cornfield Road, not only for the patrons of the tea rooms but also to stock a 'mobile shop' which toured neighbouring villages. This was driven by Miss Connie Brewer of Seaford (on the left in the lower photograph), one of the first women in the district to drive a commercial vehicle. The building was destroyed by an air raid on 7 March 1943.

Nellie Bowman (right) and her sister Isa were child actresses who appeared in the first stage presentation of *Alice in Wonderland*. The author Lewis Carroll (the Revd Charles Lutwidge Dodgson) befriended them and they spent holidays with him at 7 Lushington Road, where he stayed every summer from 1876 to 1897. Miss Bowman said she could never remember a time when she was not on the stage. She played Donna Filomena in a translation of the Spanish comedy *El Centenario* ('A Hundred Years Old') first at the Lyric Theatre, Hammersmith, and then in the touring company that visited the Devonshire Park Theatre in March 1929.

The staff of Bobby's Restaurant. The store in Terminus Road had a well-appointed restaurant on the top floor. In 1959 the large complement of waiters, waitresses and other staff was under the supervision of manageress Miss Sargent (in dark dress).

Sandy Powell – 'Mr Eastbourne'. At the age of 5 Albert Arthur Powell (nicknamed 'Sandy' from his hair colour) was helping with his mother's marionette act. At 9 he was on stage as a soprano, using his older cousin's birth certificate, since the law forbade performers under 11. He began a life-long association with pantomime six years later, and played in 'Fred Karno's Football Team' in 1920. He was heard on the wireless from its earliest days – his catch-phrase 'Can you hear me, Mother?' began as a fill-in when he dropped his script during a spoof commentary *Sandy at the North Pole* – and appeared in the first television variety show in 1932. For twenty years, until fire destroyed the Pier Theatre on 8 January 1970, he presented seasonal shows and concerts there, and lived just around the corner in Elms Avenue with his wife, Kay.

In wartime every piece of available land was used for agricultural purposes and women found themselves doing jobs traditionally reserved for men. This view shows harvesting in progress on the land between Milton Road and the cemetery. The 120 ft tower of St Michael and All Angels' Church, built in 1901, is on the right.

CHURCHES

All Souls' Church. Built in 1882 with money given by Lady Victoria Wellesley, great-niece of the Duke of Wellington, the church is in Italian Romanesque style, as are the vicarage and church hall on the left. The area was originally marshland and the church foundations were said to be as deep as the church is tall. In the foreground is Longstone Road, named after one of the Duke of Devonshire's estates in Derbyshire.

St Mary's Church was built in the twelfth century on the site of a Saxon church dedicated to St Michael. The Norman tower is made of Eastbourne greensand, quarried from a site near the present Queens Hotel. This unusual view of the church was produced by D.R. Duncan & Co. of Terminus Road in 1905. The majority of the tombstones in this picture have now been cleared.

St Mary's Church interior. Like many twelfth-century churches, St Mary's was built with a chancel at a slight angle to the nave, representing Christ's head leaning to one side on the cross. On the wall of the south aisle is a memorial to Henry Lushington, which tells the interesting story of his life in the East, including how he survived the 'Black Hole of Calcutta'.

The Salvation Army Band, 1904. It is hard to imagine the Salvation Army Band as lawbreakers but in the 1890s they insisted on marching through the town on a Sunday, contrary to the local by-laws and to the great annoyance of local people. The resulting disturbances (on one occasion involving 7,000 people) led to the formation of the Eastbourne Borough Police, and it took the House of Lords to amend the regulations to allow the band to march in peace. This photograph shows the band outside their Langney Road Citadel.

St Anne's Church. Located in Upperton Gardens, this church was the work of local architect H.S. Spurrell and was built in 1882. It was destroyed by incendiary bombs during the war and the remains were finally demolished in 1955.

The Congregational Church stood at the corner of Pevensey Road and Cavendish Place. It was closed and sold in 1973 to provide funds for St Barnabas' Church in Kingfisher Drive, Langney. The building was demolished in 1977.

Baptist Church, opened in 1871. Before this, Baptist worship had taken place at the Leaf Hall. In April 1943 this row of houses, including Lyndhurst House (where the maid is looking out), was bombed. Six girls sheltering under the stairs at no. 8, next to the church, were pulled out of the rubble alive, but the church was closed for five years for repairs.

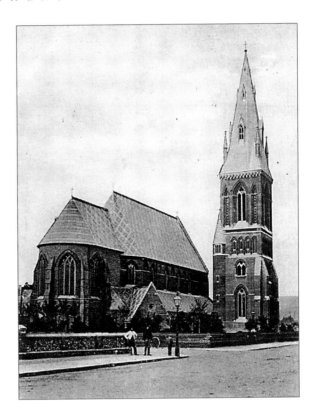

St Saviour's Church was built in 1867 on land given by the Duke of Devonshire. The almost free-standing tower was added in 1872 and is 175 ft high. The altar was made by the Pre-Raphaelite wood carver, George Jack, a pupil of William Morris. Pevsner described the building as 'particularly fine', but Sir John Betjeman thought it 'a splendid boiler'.

St Peter's Church. A temporary chapel was built on the corner of Granville Road and Meads Road in 1878. The church was rebuilt in 1894 to a design by Henry Currey who was also responsible for the Winter Gardens and Devonshire Park Theatre. Pevsner was impressed by the five-stepped lancet windows above the altar which this view shows well. Although a listed building, it was made redundant and demolished in 1971.

Summerdown Camp Church Parade. In late 1915 the camp band was under the baton of Bandmaster W.J. McConnell and included musicians from twenty-four different regiments. On Sundays they led the parade of convalescents to local churches in the morning, and in the afternoon (3 to 4 p.m.) played in the pier bandstand.

The New Congregational Church was designed by Hastings architect H. Ward and built on the site of a blacksmith's forge. The foundation stones were laid in 1903. It is pictured here shortly after its opening, and before Haynes undertakers was built on the left in 1905.

A group of dissenting soldiers billeted in Eastbourne towards the end of the eighteenth century hired a room at Seahouses for their worship. By 1809 this group had grown and purchased a plot of land in Grove Road to build a chapel. In 1860 these Methodists leased a plot of land in Pevensey Road from the Duke of Devonshire. School buildings were later added and in 1874 the Duke donated the freehold to the Church. Greater attendances in the early years of the new century required new premises and the church and school buildings (shown here) were opened in 1908.

Situated at the southern end of Blackwater Road, this brick-built Presbyterian Church is now the United Reformed Church.

Holy Trinity Church was built in 1838 as the Trinity District Chapel. It was designed by Decimus Burton who also designed the Marble Arch and the splendid sweep of Adelaide Crescent in Hove. Unfortunately most of his original work has been lost in subsequent alterations.

St John's Church animal service, 1966. The first Animal Thanksgiving Service in Eastbourne was held at this church in Meads, on 29 September 1963. Owing to inclement weather the vicar, Revd Philip Richards, allowed the service to be held inside the church. The congregation of two hundred included cats, dogs, rabbits and even a parrot. In this picture Kevin, wearing his Willingdon Primary School blazer, looks rather concerned as a dog eyes up Walter the tortoise. Perhaps he thinks it is a meat pie!

SCHOOLDAYS

Eastbourne's sands have always been ideal for young people in the holidays to mess about with buckets and spades. Other delights included the Punch and Judy show, the Hurdy-Gurdy man and the balloon seller.

Christ Church School, 1927. The school stood on the corner of Redoubt Road and Latimer Road. In 1897 the Revd Charles Lutwidge Dodgson (better known as Lewis Carroll), addressed the staff and children of the school during what was to be his last visit to the town; he died the following year.

Christ Church School class, June 1906. Kevin's grandmother, Bessie Roberts, is on the far right of the front row. The headmaster at this time was Mr Venables, who lived in the Flint House, opposite the school.

This interior view of a classroom at Christ Church School was taken in August 1911 when Bessie Roberts was 10 years old. The following year she moved to Willowfield Council Central School. Bessie is second from the right in the third row back.

Children's Corner, Devonshire Park. The young were not forgotten in planning the sports and leisure activities offered at Devonshire Park. With access through a special gate at the corner of College Road and Blackwater Road, the playground had swings, slides, a sandpit and other amusements, including a giant draughts-board. From 1952 to 1967 the playground was managed by Mrs Eva Martin, and it closed in the 1970s.

Granville House School was situated at the corner of Gaudick Road and Carlisle Road. This was the entrance hall, which must have needed a lot of dusting, especially the stuffed crocodile on the right! Dame Jean Lena Annette Conan Doyle DBE, daughter of Sir Arthur Conan Doyle, doctor, novelist, historian and creator of Sherlock Holmes, attended the school in the 1920s. As Air Commandant Director of the Women's Auxiliary Air Force, she was an honorary aide-de-camp to Her Majesty the Queen for three years from 1963.

Queenwood School, 1 & 2 Staveley Road, c. 1903. The school from which Queenwood grew was founded at Caen in Normandy in 1862. It was relocated across the Channel in 1871 at Hyde Gardens and three years later moved into two houses in Wilmington Gardens. The name 'Queenwood' was adopted when 1 Staveley Road was occupied in 1890; eight years later the neighbouring property was acquired, the buildings being connected by a glassed-in corridor. Originally the school had twenty-six girl pupils, but numbers increased until in 1905 larger premises had to be found in Darley Road.

THE CLIFF, EASTBOURNE.

Formerly Earp's Mansion, Cliff School was situated at a prominent site off St John's Road. The publishers of this postcard, G. & R. Lavis, advertised in the 1881 Gowland's *Directory* as 'Photographers and Miniature Painters to Her Majesty' and had studios in Terminus Road and in Regent Street, London.

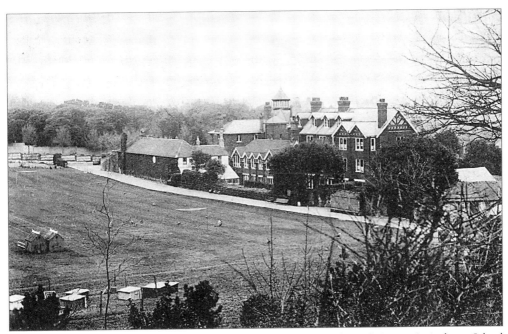

St Andrews School, 1915. Situated at the junction of Darley Road and Meads Street, St Andrews School was founded in 1877 on the site of Colstocks Farm. The barn and granary of the farm can be seen on the left of the school buildings.

Clovelly-Kepplestone, *c.* 1910. This college for girls, some of whom referred to their school as 'Clo-Kep', was formed by the merger in 1905 of Clovelly Ladies' School and Kindergarten, with Kepplestone Ladies' School, at premises in Staveley Road. In the 1920s, when Mrs Frances Anne Browne was principal, there were about 150 pupils. It closed in 1935.

Gilbert Lake, Princes Park. A favourite pastime for Eastbourne children for many years has been sailing toy yachts or using pedalos on the lake at Princes Park. Mr Gilbert-Davies gave 28 acres of land to the town in order to form the Gilbert Recreation Ground. Unemployed men topped the shingle of this area of the Crumbles with ballast and top soil. When the Prince of Wales (later the Duke of Windsor) planted a tree here during a visit to the town in 1931 the name was changed to Princes Park (although the printers of this postcard have mis-spelt the name!).

SPORT & ENTERTAINMENT

From 1875, when the famous Wimbledon Croquet Club converted one of its lawns into a tennis court, leading to the foundation of the annual tennis championship, the game became popular with middle-class families. Usually a lawn was already available, there were no problems with organizing large teams, the equipment needed was simple, and the social aspect appealed to young people in an era of restrictions and formalities. Tennis was considered a suitable game for young ladies, and many schools added it to their outdoor curriculum. In this lantern slide group photograph by Ellis Kelsey (believed to be at Greencroft School) several girls hold racquets: are they dreaming of becoming a second Lottie Dod, who won her first Wimbledon title in 1887 at the age of 15?

The Eastbourne Municipal Band. The town's first permanent orchestra was formed in 1874, and engagements included performances at Devonshire Park in its early days. In 1898 the corporation formed the 27-piece municipal orchestra, engaging conductor/composer Theo Ward (left) at a salary of £350 per annum. Said by friends to be 'music-mad', he held the position for some ten years, in which time the Winter Gardens, the pier and the seafront bandstand were among concert venues, as suggested by the parade of 'mashers' in the caricature below.

Running along the centre of the pier is a cast-iron windbreak, painted in silver with dolphin designs picked out in red, which was added in 1903. Within a few years the bandstand was also built and was the venue for various bands and other forms of entertainment, such as minstrels and pierrots.

Eastbourne Bicycle Club.			Season, 1900. Run Card.		
Date	Start	For		Miles out	Light up at
Aug. 1	6 p.m	Practising in Devonshire Park, for those who have entered for Race Meeting ...			8.47
,, 8	6 p.m.	Jevington *via* Stones Cross		8	8.35
,, 15	3 p.m.	Berwick *via* Polegate		10	8.22
,, 22	4 p.m.	Proposed Lawn Dance to meet Bexhill C.C....		4½	8.8
,, 29	6 p.m.	Chiddingly *via* Polegate		12	7.53
Sept. 5	3p.m.	Firle, Lawn Dance (by kind invitation of the Lewes C. C.)		13	7.37
,, 12	6 p.m.	Golden Cross *via* Lower Road		12	7.5
,, 19	3 p.m.	Gardner Street, Tea at the Woolpack ...		12	6.49
,, 26	6 p.m.	Horsebridge		9	6.33
Oct. 3		LAST RUN, arrangements later			

RULES.—Runs not to exceed more than **10 miles** an hour.
WHISTLE : 1 Stop, 2 Slow up, 3 Start
Special Notice given of any other Fixtures that may be arranged. These Runs are subject to alteration.
Start from Fountain top of Devonshire Place **J. Niedermayer,** *Captain*
Head Quarters GILDRIDGE HOTEL   Annual Subscription, Gentlemen 5/-, Ladies 3/6
Colours. LIGHT AND DARK BLUE   Entrance Fee,   2/6, ,,   1/6

The Bicycle Club, 1900. The club's headquarters at this time was the Gildredge Hotel, which still stands in Terminus Road by the railway station, though it was severely damaged in an air raid in February 1940. On the occasion of King Edward VII's visit in July 1903 (*see* p. 48), the club erected a triumphal arch at the junction of Lushington Road and Hyde Gardens. Several bicycles, together with a representation of the borough coat of arms, were suspended on a framework of silver poles, and garlanded with 250 yards of evergreen.

Devonshire Park and Baths, 1874. The land for the park was given by the 7th Duke of Devonshire because he wished to close the town's cricket ground for redevelopment; the new park used turf from the old cricket ground. Opened on 1 July 1874, the park soon became Eastbourne's main site of entertainment and recreation.

The skating rink was opened exactly a year after the park. Displays of 'ornamental skating' were given by Mr J.C. Plimpton, who invented the roller skate. Skating was not confined to daylight hours: note the overhanging lamps and strings of fairy lights.

This view from 1906 shows the croquet lawns with tables nearby set for afternoon tea. The towers of the Devonshire Park Theatre and of the swimming baths dominate the skyline.

A new stand opened in June 1996 in time for the annual ladies' tennis championships at Devonshire Park which has long been a favourite venue for top tennis players to 'warm up' prior to Wimbledon. Tennis tournaments have been held here since 1881.

DEVONSHIRE PARK

Manager and Secretary   ...   ...   EDGAR ALLAN BROWN.

ORCHESTRAL CONCERTS DAILY.

Musical Director—NORFOLK MEGONE.

MONDAY, TUESDAY & WEDNESDAY (Sept. 27th, 28th & 29th),

Miss LILA FIELD'S

Celebrated London Company of English Girl Dancers.

Saturday Evening, October 2nd,

Madame REJANE.

IN THE PAVILION.

EVERY EVENING at 8.   Matinees: Wednesday & Saturday at 3.15

These two photographs illustrate some of the Devonshire Park attractions during the First World War. As well as daily concerts by the Devonshire Park orchestra and guest appearances by the Summerdown Convalescent Camp band and entertainers, programmes included cinematograph showings of silent movies starring Charlie Chaplin or West End actor Lewis Waller, news pictures of Lord Kitchener's visit to the Front, and lantern slide lectures such as *With Joffre and the French*. In the autumn/winter of 1915/16 alone, the exiled Belgian violinst Eugène Ysaÿe, accompanied by his pianist brother Théo, the Russian pianist Vladimir Pachmann, the London theatre producer Charles Hawtrey, the English contralto Clara Butt and the renowned Parisienne comedy actress Madame Gabrielle Réjane (left) all appeared at the hall.

Devonshire Park Theatre
EASTBOURNE
Monday, Jan 21. FEB Six Nights at 8
Matinees Wednesday and Saturday at 2.30

MR. HORACE HODGES
"GRUMPY"

By Horace Hodges and T. Wigney Percyval

By arrangement with
MR. CYRIL MAUDE

Many West End plays visited the Devonshire Park Theatre on their provincial tours. The role of 'Grumpy' had been played by Cyril Maude in London and North America but at Eastbourne it was taken by Horace Hodges, the joint author of the play.

York Road gymnasium, 1906. The gym was at 20 York Road, off Grove Road, and in 1895 this well-equipped room, fitted with plenty of ropes and ladders, was run by Mr C. Moss. This card was sent by Gladys to a friend in Rochester, New York State. She wrote: 'This is the place we have gymnastics in once a week and I do enjoy it so much.'

The New Picture Hall in Seaside Road (above) was opened by the Duke of Devonshire in 1879. It later became the headquarters of the Eastbourne Conservative Society (1886) and the Constitutional Club (1897). The first films were shown here in about 1906; the building later became the Tivoli Cinema and remained in use until September 1982. In 1925 it showed *The Kid* (left), starring Charlie Chaplin. Kevin's grandmother Bessie Gordon made a point of attending the last showing (*The French Lieutenant's Woman*), as her brother-in-law Reg ('The Boss') had been the projectionist here for over twenty-five years. The projectionist at this final showing was John Starkey on his 36th birthday.

Bobby's Restaurant. Musical accompaniment to meals was common in larger restaurants before the Second World War. Alfredo's Magyar Quartet, as photographed by F.A. Bourne of Langley Road, entertained patrons of Bobby's (*see* p. 55).

Bobby's Revue, 1961. The talented staff at Bobby's department store presented an annual show at the Winter Gardens. This scene from their 1961 show, *Cabaret Time*, produced by Pat Bodle, included Glenna Gasson, Avril Langridge and Graham Tubb.

The full cast of Bobby's Revue takes a bow at the end of Pat Bodle's 1962 production at the Winter Gardens. The cast includes Stella Dench, Avril Langridge, Beryl Newsome, Rebecca Shingles, Joan Sully, Michael Johnson and Graham Tubb.

BUILDINGS

Queens Hotel. Two thousand years ago there was a Roman villa with its own pavement bath here; the foundations were discovered in 1712. The present hotel was built by Henry Currey and opened in June 1880, apparently as a visual barrier between the 'posh' hotels to the west and the more modest boarding houses of the eastern parade. This photograph was taken prior to the extension of the west wing.

Motcombe farmhouse, 1911. This area was the site of the original Anglo-Saxon settlement. Motcombe farmhouse is a Georgian-style, nineteenth-century building, with fine coursed cobblestones, which replaced an earlier farm. Two other farm buildings can be seen in the gardens opposite: the old barn which has now been converted into cottages, and the round dovecote which provided food during winter months.

The Lamb Hotel. Still run by Harvey's Brewery of Lewes, the Lamb is Eastbourne's oldest pub. The name has religious connotations and the building may have been a resting place for pilgrims. In the nineteenth century fashionable balls were held here in the 'large room', which was the only indoor place for meetings in the parish. In 1852 Dr Darling gave a lecture here on 'Spirit-rapping, table turning and mesmerism', during which a tremendous storm occurred and many people ran away frightened, calling the doctor 'satanic'. The plaster on the front of the building was removed in 1912. The sign on the corner of Ocklynge Road points to John Dukes clothing and boot stores at no. 14 and the poster on the extreme right advertises a visit by Miss Lila Field's girl dancers (see p. 76).

Old Town post office, Star Road. The post office has occupied a number of locations to the rear of the Lamb Inn. Until 1880 it was sited in a small cottage on the eastern side of Ocklynge Road, and the postmaster was John Payne. He died in 1880 and his wife Hannah became official postmistress in the new premises in Star Road. Later generations of the Payne family also served the Post Office in Eastbourne.

Compton Place. Originally called Bourne Place, this is Eastbourne's only Grade I listed building. In 1724 the house was purchased by Spencer Compton, Earl of Wilmington and Speaker of the House of Commons. He had the house remodelled and later, in 1800, the four-arch Tuscan porch was added. Inset is the 8th Duke of Devonshire who was Mayor of Eastbourne in 1897 and 1898. As a child he remembered 'walking from Compton Place to the Wish Tower by a footpath through fields of waving corn'. The seaside home of the Dukes of Devonshire, Compton Place has welcomed many distinguished guests including Edward VIII, George V and Queen Mary, and our present Queen. After the 10th Duke died in 1950, the house was closed until 1954 when it reopened as a School of English.

The Indian Pavilion. This exotic building was originally built at Chelsea by the P&O Steamship Company for the Royal Naval Exhibition of 1892. It was later moved into Devonshire Park where it was used as a refreshment room until it was demolished in 1963 to make way for the Congress Theatre.

The Winter Gardens. Called on this picture 'The Pavilion', the Winter Gardens were designed by Henry Currey and formed the main entrance into Devonshire Park. Described as 'a miniature Crystal Palace', the building was used as a ballroom and concert hall. Luggage porters with their hand-barrows wait for business in Compton Street while on the extreme right can be seen Tower House. This was built in 1886 as a residence for the Devonshire Park manager and since 1982 has been the home of the Eastbourne Heritage Centre, which contains a fascinating museum of the town's history.

Devonshire Park Theatre. Viewed here from Lascelles House, the theatre was another building designed by Henry Currey, although the interior was remodelled by theatre architect Frank Matcham in 1903. The theatre held its first performance on 4 June 1884 and it is said to be haunted by a ghostly violinist. During the Second World War the theatre was kept running by ENSA (Entertainments National Services Association) and operated by Royal Navy personnel.

The Technical Institute was opened in August 1904 by the Dowager Duchess of Devonshire. The building housed a school of art, a library and a museum. At 11.30 a.m. on Friday 4 June 1943 it received a direct hit during an air raid on the town by eighteen German bombers. The site was used for the new public library which opened in April 1964.

Believed to be the first purpose-built convalescent hospital in the country, All Saints Hospital was built for the 'All Saints Sisters of the Poor', founded in London in 1851 by Harriet Brownlow-Byron. Mother Harriet became ill in 1862 and came to Eastbourne to recover. Built between 1867 and 1869, the building is in Victorian High Gothic style, and made of brick, stone and tiles. The houses on the right are in Cliff Road. Note the two ladies who have stopped for a breather, en route to Beachy Head.

Homeopathic Hospital, 1907. Sited at 36 Enys Road on the corner of Carew Road, this hospital was opened in 1888 as a convalescent home for women. The aim of the hospital was to 'provide a temporary seaside home for debilitated people whose restoration is effected by pure air, rest and a good diet'. This picture was published by the London-based Scientific Press who specialized in hospital postcards!

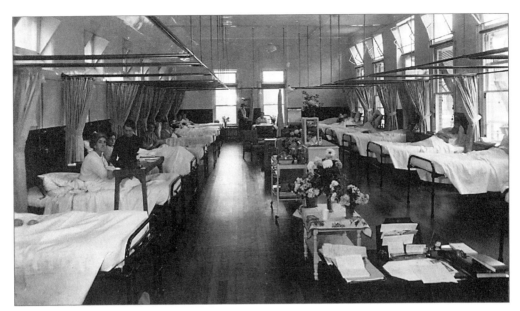

The Princess Alice Hospital. Princess Alice was the second daughter of Queen Victoria. She suffered from ill-health and came to Eastbourne to convalesce but died, aged only 35, in 1878. Five years later the hospital was opened by the Prince of Wales. The photograph above shows the Geraldine Ward. During the 1930s the hospital dealt with over 1,700 in-patients and 20,000 out-patients each year, and the hospital had to advertise for subscribers and donations. Events like the children's fancy dress ball shown below helped to raise funds. The hospital closed in May 1996.

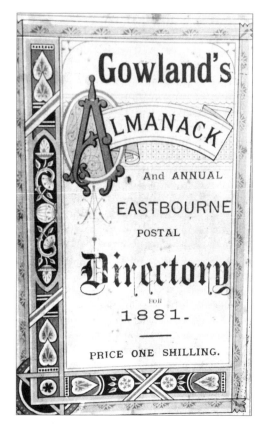

Another of Kevin's great-great-uncles was Bert Bennett, who was a printer. He started off working for Gowland's who published an annual town almanac, shown on the left. This offered a plethora of information including tide-tables, railway fares and postage rates and collection times, as well as a full street directory and a diary. Bert later opened his own premises at 24 Church Street near St Mary's Church from where he printed, among other things, the *Summerdown Camp Journal* from which many of the pictures in the 'Military' section of this book have been reproduced.

This view, looking north-east from the spire of St Saviour's Church, is a reproduction of a photograph taken in the 1860s. On the upper left can be seen the railway station and the line curving around towards Polegate. Lushington Road and Hyde Gardens are in the foreground, with the tall houses of Sussex Gardens on the upper right. These buildings, now above the Arndale Centre, can still be seen from the pedestrianized part of Terminus Road.

Oak Cabin Restaurant. Pat remembers how, during childhood holidays, she would ask her parents to take her to what she called 'the railway train' restaurant, because of its carriage-like interior. This licensed restaurant was the venue for wedding receptions and similar events.

Beachy Head Hotel, 1948. This building on top of Beachy Head was once called the Queens Hotel. The poet Rupert Brooke stayed here with his mother during visits to the town. It was damaged by fire in the 1920s and 1960s and in December 1994 was completely burnt to the ground. It has now been rebuilt as a pub. Nearby there is a visitor centre giving information about the natural history of the local downland.

The Watch Tower, 1933. Lloyds of London began signalling at Beachy Head in 1877 when they leased the Watch Tower from the Duke of Devonshire. It was rebuilt in 1896 and purchased outright the following year. In 1904 Lloyds transferred signalling to the nearby Coastguard Cottages and the tower became a kiosk, selling postcards and films.

Coastguard Cottages, 1914. These houses look more like a row of suburban terracing than a coastguard station 500 ft above sea level on top of one of the most famous parts of Britain's coastline. It consisted of the naval station on the left and five cottages, which must have had to contend with some appalling weather.

Beachy Head, 1914. This view shows all the previous three buildings. The coastguard cottages appear to have walled back gardens. The noticeboard behind the two ladies probably warns visitors about the dangers of getting too close to the ever-crumbling cliffs. How did their hats stay on!

Aerial view of Eastbourne. All Souls' Church is on the left. The Queens Hotel is in the foreground and behind, towards the rear of the town, the Bedfordwell Waterworks can be seen. On the far right are the whitewashed buildings of Seahouses. Alfred, Lord Tennyson stayed here and enjoyed his visit, but the essayist Charles Lamb left, complaining that Eastbourne was 'dull'. Charles Darwin was another visitor to Seahouses in the 1850s whilst working on his book, *The Origin of Species*.

The Glastonbury Hotel, 1911. Situated at 4–9 Royal Parade, the hotel has been running since the turn of the century. The domestic staff are posed on the balcony with, perhaps, the proprietors on the right and a bed-ridden lady reading a paper behind the wrought-iron hotel sign. Guests, some in holiday rig, pose on the steps.

The San Remo Hotel, which is still trading, overlooks the sea from 39–43 Royal Parade. When this photograph was taken some time in the 1920s, Mesdames Dale were the proprietors.

Ratton Manor. Lord and Lady Willingdon lived here for many years, becoming part of the village community. 'The Squire' served as Viceroy of India, Governor of Canada and Governor of Madras, and was a personal friend of King George V. His wife Marie was renowned for the magnificent gardens she established and her head gardener, Mr Leach, was invited to be a judge at Summerdown Convalescent Camp's flower shows.

YWCA at Westdown. The Young Women's Christian Association was established 'to promote world-wide fellowship and understanding of the Christian faith, to advance education and welfare particularly among young people'. Its modern work includes the running of 'hostels, youth clubs, nearly-new shops, and family and health workshops'. Its Eastbourne hostel was at 4 Hartington Place (on the corner of Compton Street), next door to Holy Trinity parsonage. The Devonshire Club now occupies the site.

Happy days at Westdown.

SECTION TEN

MILITARY

EASTBOURNE.

The Redoubt Fortress was built between 1804 and 1810 to counter Napoleon's threats of invasion. During the Napoleonic War up to two hundred soldiers were based here, although in the long run it was the sea rather than 'old Boney' that posed the greater threat; in 1867 the War Department had to spend £10,000 on the surrounding sea wall. In 1925 the council bought the building and it has since housed a model village, an aquarium and, more recently, the Combined Services Museum.

The Royal Sussex Regiment Memorial. Unveiled in 1906 (*see* p. 50), the memorial stands 20 ft high and depicts a young officer of the 2nd Battalion of the Royal Sussex Regiment before the Indian Mutiny. The regiment was raised in 1701 and served in Gibraltar during the Napoleonic Wars and in New York City during the American Wars of Independence. Four Victoria Crosses were awarded to Royal Sussex men during the First World War. In 1951 the regiment was awarded the freedom of Eastbourne and in June 1966 it became part of the Queen's Regiment.

Eastbourne Cadet Force. These lads are probably a school company, posing with their officers and the clergy of St Mary's Church before the First World War. They are in front of the distinctive porch of the vicarage in Vicarage Road.

The Surrey Brigade Camp, July 1912. More than 3,000 men of the Surrey Infantry Brigade and Army Service Corps (Territorial Army) arrived in Eastbourne by special train and set up camp for a week at Whitbread Hollow above Meads. It was believed to be the largest concentration of troops on the south coast since the days of the threatened Napoleonic invasion. Fresh water was laid on from Eastbourne Waterworks at Friston. The commanding officer was Colonel W.G. Caith and on the Sunday a church parade was held with massed bands and visitors.

Summerdown Military Convalescent Camp was opened in early 1915 to accommodate some of the soldiers recovering from wounds received in the fighting on the Western Front and (later) in the Dardanelles campaign. The camp occupied an area bounded today by Old Camp Road, Compton Drive and Pashley Road.

Christmas greetings, 1915. This novelty card, bearing the regimental badge of the Royal Artillery, was sent by Sergeant-Major and Mrs Larman, then living at Providence House, 37 Whitley Road. The verse inside reads: 'Our flag still stands for freedom, For honour, truth and right, And Britain's sons have proved anew, Her majesty and might.'

The Welcome Hut, Summerdown Camp. Adjoining the orderly room, the Welcome Hut was run by a committee of local ladies. With a record of providing meals 'at all hours of the day', the hut gave a warm and friendly first impression of the camp to wounded men arriving after their long and sometimes painful journeys.

Summerdown Camp had been in existence for only a few months before it became necessary to enlarge the Welcome Hut.

Summerdown Massage Institute. At the start of the First World War, Compton Place was the home of Mrs Almeric Paget who, with War Office approval, formed, equipped and maintained a corps of fifty trained masseuses. By July 1915 these ladies, whose numbers grew to five hundred, were at work in the London, Eastbourne, Dartford and Epsom convalescent units. In the first three months, nearly 2,000 cases were treated at Eastbourne. In spite of alarming poems and concert-party allusions to the treatment they received, the patients genuinely appreciated the work which aided their recovery.

A Blue Boy, 1918. In their shapeless bright blue jackets and trousers, smartened by the white facings and shirt, red tie and distinguishing regimental headgear, the wounded soldiers soon became part of Eastbourne's wartime community. Local people generously donated books, gramophone records, plants, games equipment, musical instruments, tobacco and craft materials. The men were welcomed into neighbouring homes, and many friendships (and several marriages!) resulted. Jack Sealy of the 6th South Wales Borderers recorded his gratitude to Kevin's great-grandparents with this self-portrait.

A football committee, chaired by the chaplain, organized games at an informal six-a-side level for convalescents, leading on to more serious inter-camp teams playing league matches against the Royal Naval Air Service, Royal Sussex Regiment, Hants Carabineers, and other neighbouring units. At appropriate times of the year, the men could also play cricket and golf and take part in sea-fishing competitions. This photograph has been produced from one of Ellis Kelsey's lantern slides.

The catering team was so highly regarded by the convalescents that poems were written about them, and the camp pantomime *Babes in the Wood* had a scene in 'the lady cooks' orderly room', featuring Corporal Oliver Crombie as the 'dame'. The joke was taken in good part by the genuine cooks in the audience. The camp journal reported that at Christmas 1915 the ladies staged a cookery demonstration as part of the camp fête, and although they roasted turkeys and made mince pies for dinner on 25 December, the plum puddings were supplied by Harrods.

In Summerdown, as in any army camp, cookhouse and other fatigues had to be done. Food figured largely in the comic poems and other writings that appeared in the camp magazine. Gifts of fruit and vegetables came in from local people, and at Christmas 1915 His Majesty King George V sent pheasants from his estate, and the Mayor and Mayoress of Eastbourne provided a very large cake. There were also various references to tea-parties, theatre outings and other hospitality events organized by local residents for the convalescents in their midst.

Lieutenant-Colonel J.S. Bostock, RAMC.
As Major Bostock, he had been in charge of
a convalescent camp for the sick and lightly
wounded in France. Greatly respected by
one and all, he was promoted and given the
task of establishing the larger Summerdown
Camp in 1915.

Medal presentations, June 1916.
Brigadier-General the Earl of
Shaftesbury (left) presents the
Distinguished Conduct Medal to
Sergeant John Kerry of the 1st
Seaforth Highlanders for bravery
in action near Givenchy. To the
right stands Company
Quartermaster Sergeant Varnham
of the 4th Middlesex Regiment,
awaiting the moment when the
Earl will present him with the
Czar's Russian Order of Saint
George, awarded for leadership
and for saving the life of a
wounded man at Mons in August
1915. CQMS Varnham already
held the Distinguished Conduct
Medal.

Visiting the camp. Family and friends were encouraged to visit the convalescents at Summerdown as a vital aid to their recovery. The tent run by the Young Men's Christian Association kept a list of suitable lodgings, all offered by householders with men in the army. A room and board could be had for about 14s per head per week. The Empire Hostel was also established at 51 Upperton Gardens, while bedrooms could be booked for 1s per night for unaccompanied lady visitors, from the matron of the Women's Hostel at 105 Latimer Road.

Relatives and friends were always welcome at the camp. Pat's grandfather, Private James Henley Washford of the Bedfordshire Regiment, was a patient at Summerdown, having been sent home from France suffering from trench-foot, a severe condition brought on by many hours' standing in rain-filled trenches. Pat's mother (then aged about 12), recalls going to visit him at Summerdown, with *her* mother and a younger sister, and staying at the home of Mrs Pocock of Green Street.

THE 4 Ks

THE BOGUS MAJOR

The Bogus Major. This farce was first presented on Thursday 2 September 1915 by the 4 Ks ('Knuts Kamp Komedy Kompany'), formed by Lieutenant E. Green-Foley RAMC in the early days of the camp. Lance-Corporal Leslie Gray played the title role, with Lance-Corporal Thomas as 'Penelope'; the camp journal reported that 'sly allusions to the lady cooks and sentences of a court martial to 28 days' massage called forth roars of laughter'. The play was written by Lance-Corporal Sizer and was repeated at a concert in October, and again the following month.

The well-attended camp gymkhana, September 1915. Privates Hutchinson and Lambert may well be inside the pantomime horse, repeating the role they played in support of Lance-Corporal Thomas's singing of *A Prairie Life for Me* at a concert the week before. Lance-Corporal Thomas as 'Summerdown Kate' (with tennis racquet), Rifleman Doherty (the clown) and Private Yardley were among those who entertained the guests, who included Lady French, wife of the Commander-in-Chief of the Army, Sir John French.

'A' Lines gardens. Gardening was one of the open-air occupations that the convalescents were encouraged to follow. Colonel Bostock invited Miss Winifred Pattisson to start things off and she regularly contributed '*Notes on Camp Gardening*' to the Summerdown Journal. Other local ladies also assisted, collecting plants and shrubs and organizing flower shows at three-weekly intervals, at which the judges were the head gardeners to the Duke of Devonshire and Lord Willingdon.

South Wales Borderers. At the start of the First World War there was great enthusiasm to join the Army and fight the war that would be 'over by Christmas'. These men would soon be kitted out in khaki and marched off for training.

LAW & ORDER

Eastbourne's own police force was founded in 1891, partly as a result of the Salvation Army disturbances (see p. 59). Policing a busy seaside town necessitated the appointment of 'Parade Inspectors' to patrol the seafront. In July 1927 the force introduced a system of police boxes, each having a telephone link to the police station in Grove Road, only the third of its kind in the country. Other new ideas tried out in Eastbourne were the use of 'give way' lines at junctions and the breathalyser, both of which were extended across the country after these trials.

'Waiting for the Barks.' A 1911 by-law forbade dogs to bark on the beach! This postcard was sent by Tom to Sid (in Barking!); he wrote: 'how dare they bark? – there's such a lot of them too, beastly horrid things, my word!' The cartoon shows the mayor and mace-bearer in full regalia, with a beach inspector and three borough constables, stalking a small dog on the beach with the Wish Tower in the background.

Latimer Road police station. This sub-station was built in 1895, together with three police houses, nos 60, 62 and 64, at a cost of £2,620 and stood at the junction of Halton Road. The 1896 Pike's *Directory* lists Sergeant Hunisett as the first 'officer in charge'; the houses were occupied by Sergeant Tugwell and Constables Cook and Compton. The station was closed in 1930, partly to fund the new police box system; however, the houses remained in police use until the mid-1930s with Sergeant W. Phillips staying on at no. 60 until 1940. The redundant police station became an orthopaedic clinic. In 1968 the building (with the porch removed) was converted into four flats; the borough crest and the date 1895 can still be seen on the first gable.

WPC Heywood.

W/Insp Saunders.

The first policewomen were employed by the railway police and in London during the First World War, but they were replaced by men when they returned home from the front. Eastbourne Borough Police became one of the first forces to employ a female officer, when Miss Heywood (left) was appointed in 1921. Prior to this, searching and dealing with female prisoners had been the responsibility of police matrons. In 1927 the Worcester Police Watch Committee was considering employing women and found that only nine forces out of the thirty-seven they contacted had policewomen. Eastbourne told them that their WPC 'holds free office of constable with power of arrest. She keeps observation upon the postcards in shops and upon clairvoyants, and does useful work amongst young girls'. The Worcester police did not follow Eastbourne's example, saying 'there are only one or two useful things a woman constable can do'. In 1927 Miss Heywood was replaced by Miss Elizabeth Saunders (right), who had served as a policewoman in a munitions factory and in the Oxford city police. She was given an office in Eastbourne Town Hall and assisted male officers in dealing with sexual offences against females; she was welcome in women's hospital wards where male officers were not. She also patrolled the town, in summer months paying special attention to the seafront, where she helped lost children. In a typical year (1931) she dealt with 161 offences, attended court on 88 occasions, took 77 statements and submitted 189 reports. She performed plain clothes duty 140 times, including checking places of amusement which she did on 93 occasions. She rose to the rank of inspector and retired from the force in 1938.

Eastbourne Borough police. This photograph, taken by the London Panoramic Company and reproduced by courtesy of the Superintendent of Eastbourne police station, shows the entire borough force in April 1926. WPC Heywood is behind the cocked hat of the Chief Constable, W.H. Smith.

FACSIMILE OF THE NOTE LEFT BY MURRAY.   (*Daris.*

A bizarre incident took place in Enys road in August 1912 when firemen attending a blaze discovered the bodies of a man, a woman and three children. One injured women, Florence Murray, escaped the flames and later an extraordinary story was revealed. The dead man was Robert Money, who also used the names Mackie and Murray. He had children by both Florence and by her sister Edith, but the sisters were unaware that he was even known to the other. When the truth came out, Money realized his hopeless situation and shot them all, and set fire to the house before turning the revolver on himself. A silver vase found in the hallway contained this note, which was reproduced in the *Daily Mail*.

Two months after the tragic events at Enys Road, a further murder rocked the town. Inspector Arthur Walls, a parade inspector of the borough force, was called to the home of Countess Sztaray in South Cliff Avenue (above) where a burglary was in progress. He called to the burglar, George Mackay (alias John Williams), to come out but the response was two shots from Mackay's revolver, which fatally wounded Arthur Walls. Mackay escaped but was later caught in London, tried and hanged. Inspector Wall's funeral was a solemn occasion attended by thousands of local people. On 16 October 1912 he was interred at Ocklynge cemetery. Gertie, who lived in South Cliff Avenue (at X), sent this card to a friend saying that it showed the scene of the crime, indicated by an asterisk.

The Crumbles. This desolate area of shingle, extending from Langney Point to Pevensey, was the scene of not one but two grisly murders in the space of less than four years. Two men were hanged for killing Irene Munro in August 1920, and then in April 1924 the town was shocked by the news that parts of a woman's body had been found at the Officer's House (above), part of the old coastguard station at Wallsend Road. Patrick Mahon was arrested, tried and convicted of the murder of Emily Beilby Kaye in spite of his protests that she had fallen in a struggle and hit her head on a coal scuttle. This is clearly visible in the official scene of crime photograph below, showing the parlour where she died. The bungalow, since demolished, became a gruesome tourist attraction and the subject of a number of postcard views.

EAST DEAN & FRISTON

Only 3 miles west of Eastbourne lies the pretty village of East Dean, which was a favourite haunt of smugglers as it was only ½ mile from the coast. The centre of the village is the Tiger Inn on the village green, and the ancient church of St Simon and St Jude nearby has an eleventh-century tower. The East Dean & Friston war memorial playing field lies on the Birling Gap road and is the home of the village cricket team.

Can you spot the different nursery rhymes illustrated by the children of East Dean School in about 1910? Standing, left to right, they represent Old Mother Hubbard, Humpty Dumpty, Jack and Jill, -?-, Simple Simon and the Pieman, Mr and Mrs Jack Spratt, -?-, Little Boy Blue. Seated: -?-, -?-, Little Bo-Peep (Isabel Dickens), Baby Bunting (Freda Curwood). The children are in the school grounds with The Hollow in the background.

This photograph shows the village laundry at the junction of Upper Street and Lower Street. Next to the laundry is 4 Upper Street which was the home of Kevin's maternal great-grandmother, Emily Dickens, for many years. Running across the picture behind the telephone wires is the Friston–Eastbourne road.

Senior pupils of East Dean School, photographed with their teacher, *c.* 1917. Kevin's maternal grandmother, Edie Dickens, is fifth from the left in the second row from the back, and on her left is Dorothy Dickens; Freda Curwood is tenth from the left in the same row.

It was a Christmastime tradition in East Dean for Santa to call on the old folk with gifts of coal and groceries. Here, young Kevin receives a present from Santa as Mr Ticehurst holds the horse. Kevin's great-grandmother looks on as his great-aunt Dorothy Dickens approaches with mince pies. This picture was taken outside the family home in Upper Street in 1950.

Friston Place. The Manor of Friston was originally owned by William Etchingham who held it by charter of Edward I. Friston Place was built in about 1540, with later additions. In 1637 it was the home of the Selwyn family whose elaborate memorials can be seen in Friston Church. For three generations it was the home of the Maitland family. This shows the eastern front of Friston Place, with the Well House on the left.

Outdoor staff, Friston Place, 1920s. This splendid group is posed by the oak front door and shows Major Francis James Maitland JP (centre) with his staff. Seated is Mrs Morris the housekeeper, and at the top right is Mr Alf West, head gardener, with his brother, Syke West, the under-gardener.

Al-fresco tea-party, 1920s. Seated, left to right nearer the camera: Mrs Morris (housekeeper), -?-, Mr Henry Curwood (valet/butler), Mrs West (head gardener's wife) with her daughter Nellie. Standing on the right are Mrs Edith Curwood (governess) and her daughter Freda.

Mr Cox lived in East Dean and worked as a road mender or 'lengthman' on the Eastbourne–East Dean road. He is seen here at the turn of the century with his shovel and barrow, and wearing well-patched clothes and hobnail boots.

Major Maitland did not want evacuees staying in his home, so when they arrived during the Second World War, he engaged the young man on the left to be their guardian, and converted an outbuilding for their use.

EASTBOURNE
BY NIGHT

Saturday night shopping.

The Avenue in winter.

Night at Ocklynge.

A wet night in Eastbourne.

A tree-lined street.

Tree shadows, 3 Devonshire Place.

A winter night, Devonshire Place.

Dripping pavements.

The Technical Institute by night.

The Albion Hotel.

Evenden's corner.

Afterglow from the pier.

ACKNOWLEDGEMENTS

Though based on Kevin's collection of photographs and family documents, and the information gleaned from them, this book has been much enhanced by advice, reminiscences, loan of pictures and other generous help from the following, here gratefully acknowledged: Mrs B. Landrock; Mr M. Lawson-Finch; Mrs P. Markquick; Mr G. Tubb; Mrs M. Turvey; Mr M. Wheatley; Mrs E. Worsfold; Eastbourne Police Scenes of Crime department; Eastbourne Reference Library; Eastbourne Heritage Centre; the Lifeboat Museum; Seaford Museum (especially for the use of the Ellis Kelsey slides); and the staff of Royal Mail and Boots the chemist, Seaford.

Special thanks are due to our families for thier support and forbearance: Mandy, Jean and Roger Gordon; Sheila Thrower; Susan Berry and Edith Tietjen.

We have done our best to obtain permission to use any material still under copyright, and apologize for any source not fully cleared or acknowledged. A note to the publishers will ensure that future editions will include any such acknowledgement.

Sources

Armstrong, Robert, *Guide to Eastbourne*

——, *Wings over Eastbourne*

Cullen, Dorothy P., *Many Years, Many Girls*

Eastbourne Civic Society, *Eight Town Walks*

Eastbourne Local History Society, various publications

Hodges, Peter R., *Temple of Dreams*

Stanley, Harry, *Can you hear me, Mother?*

Whitaker's Almanac

Wilton, John & Smith, John, *Eastbourne in old Picture Postcards*, vol. 2

Young, Kenneth, *Music's Great Days in the Spas and Watering Places*

The Summerdown Camp Journal, 1915–16